Shadows on the wall

Noises down the hall

Life doesn't frighten me at all

Bad dogs barking loud

Big ghosts in a cloud

Life doesn't frighten me at all

Mean old Mother Goose

Lions on the loose

They don't frighten me at all

Dragons breathing flame

On my counterpane

That doesn't frighten me at all.

I go boo

Make them shoo

I make fun

Way they run

I won't cry

So they fly

I just smile

They go wild

Life doesn't frighten me at all.

Tough guys fight

All alone at night

Life doesn't frighten me at all.

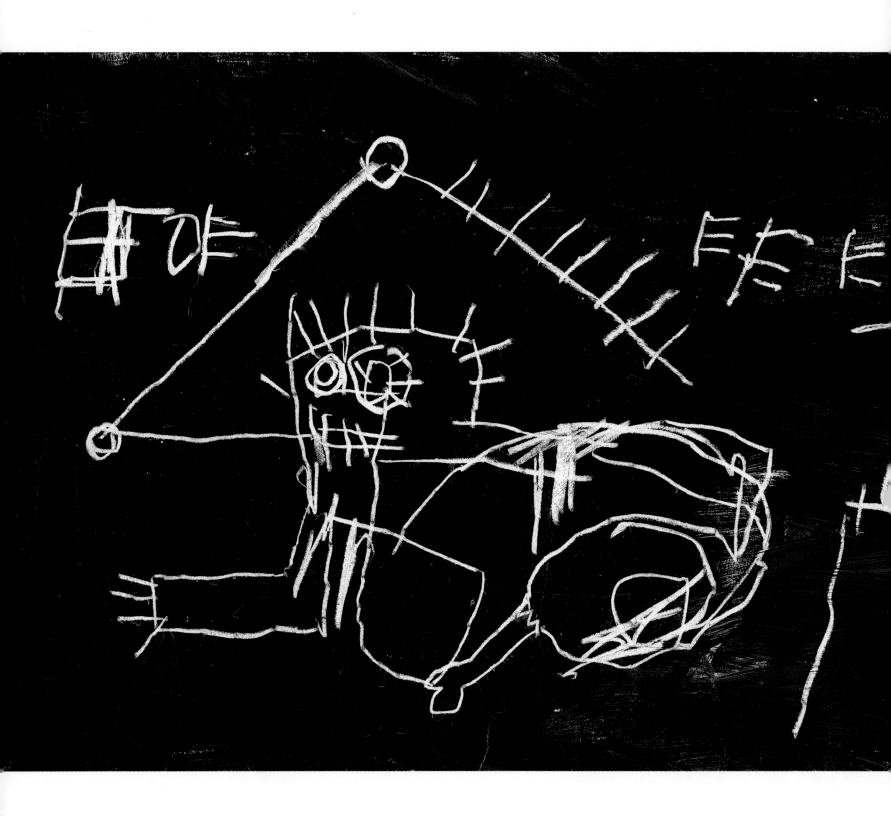

Panthers in the park

Strangers in the dark

No, they don't frighten me at all.

That new classroom where

Boys all pull my hair

(Kissy little girls

With their hair in cur(s)

They don't frighten me at all.

Don't show me frogs and snakes
And listen for my scream,
If I'm afraid at all
It's only in my dreams.

I've got a magic charm

That I keep up my sleeve,

Don't show me frogs and snakes
And listen for my scream,
If I'm afraid at all
It's only in my dreams.

I've got a magic charm

That I keep up my sleeve,

BIRTH OF EARTH©

I can walk the ocean floor

And never have to breathe.

Life doesn't frighten me at all

Not at all

Not at all.

Life doesn't frighten me at all.

Maya Angelou

Maya Angelou stands as a thriving, proud example of a modern American woman. Born in 1928 in St. Louis, Missouri, in her early childhood she experienced many traumas: parental divorce, separation from her parents, rape, poverty, and racial hatred. In her teens, she lacked the opportunity for a higher education, was denied employment on the basis of race, and while herself still a child, became a new mother. Armed with the nurturing of her grandmother, mother, and brother, and her ability for expression and participation, Angelou has done much more than merely survive.

After her parents separated when she was three, Angelou went with her older brother to live with their grandmother in Stamps, Arkansas, where race relations had little improved since the Civil War. Against this backdrop, Angelou and her brother were raised in an upright, practical, and proud family,

headed by their grandmother and influenced by the world of literature: Paul Laurence Dunbar, Langston Hughes, W. E. B. DuBois, the Brontës, Mark Twain, and Shakespeare.

When Angelou was a young teenager, she and her brother left Stamps to live with their mother in San Francisco. There, while still in school, she fought to become the first African-American "conductorette" on San Francisco's street cars, and won. She graduated from high school and soon thereafter, at the age of sixteen, bore a son. To support herself and her infant, she worked as a cook, waitress, singer, and actress.

In addition to her stage career, Angelou became increasingly involved in civil rights. From 1959–60, she was the Northern Coordinator in Dr. Martin Luther King, Jr.'s Southern Christian Leadership

Conference (SCLC). She then met a South African freedom fighter and traveled with him to England, Egypt, and Ghana. When their relationship ended, she stayed in Africa, becoming the first woman editor of the Cairo English-language news weekly and, later, a professor at the University of Ghana. Returning to the United States in the late 1960s, she continued to fight for human rights, including those of African-Americans and women.

Currently, Angelou is a professor of American studies at Wake Forest University in Winston-Salem, North Carolina. Exercising her determination to better society and its inhabitants, she continues to write passionately, lecture throughout the world, and perform her songs, poems, and stories. She also writes, produces, acts, and directs for television and the live stage. She is the recipient of many honorary degrees from colleges and universities and of countless awards and nominations, including several presidential appointments. Joining Robert Frost as the only other poet ever so honored, in 1993, Angelou was invited to compose and read a poem at the inaugural swearing-in ceremony of the President of the United States. Her advice to writers, to everyone, is to read everything possible, be it African-American, European, Latin, or other literature—but, especially Shakespeare.

With eloquence and immediacy, Maya Angelou has described her life in a series of autobiographies, beginning with the acclaimed I KNOW WHY THE CAGED BIRD SINGS. In them, as in LIFE DOESN'T FRIGHTEN ME, she shares her passion, exuberance, trials, and triumphs, so that all may feel her vitality, humor, and faith. Life, she feels, is one's sole possession, and it certainly does not frighten Maya Angelou.

SELECTED BIBLIOGRAPHY OF MAYA ANGELOU'S BOOKS:

I KNOW WHY THE CAGED BIRD SINGS. *New York: Random House, 1970.*

JUST GIVE ME A COOL DRINK OF WATER 'FORE I DIIIE. *New York: Random House, 1971.*

GATHER TOGETHER IN MY NAME. *New York: Random House, 1974.*

OH PRAY MY WINGS ARE GONNA FIT ME WELL. *New York: Random House, 1975.*

SINGIN' AND SWINGIN' AND GETTIN' MERRY LIKE CHRISTMAS. *New York: Random House, 1976.*

AND STILL I RISE. *New York: Random House, 1978.*

THE HEART OF A WOMAN. *New York: Random House, 1981.*

SHAKER, WHY DON'T YOU SING? *New York: Random House, 1983.*

ALL GOD'S CHILDREN NEED TRAVELING SHOES. *New York: Random House, 1986.*

NOW SHEBA SINGS THE SONG. *New York: E. P. Dutton, 1987.*

I SHALL NOT BE MOVED. *New York: Random House, 1990.*

Jean-Michel Basquiat

Born in 1960, Jean-Michel Basquiat was raised in a middle-class Brooklyn neighborhood in the city of New York. His Haitian father was an accountant and his Puerto Rican mother was a graphic designer. During his childhood, his parents introduced him to art, music, and theater in visits to Manhattan.

From the time the artist was four years old, he drew incessantly. All of his life, he filled notebooks with poetry, short stories, cartoons, drawings, and music. He played musical instruments and was never without music in the background, whether it was Johann Sebastian Bach, or jazz, rock, and rap.

As Basquiat grew into his teens, the sights and sounds of New York City fascinated him. He rebelled against his family and chose to become an artist. In his late teens, Basquiat left for Manhattan where he lived the traditional artist's life—1980s style—selling postcards and T-shirts on the streets and painting with a fury.

He began his artistic career drawing and lettering on building walls—just graffiti to some people, but art to others. With a friend, he created the "tag," or street name, of SAMO©, and soon SAMO©'s poetry could be seen throughout lower Manhattan and Brooklyn. Later, as the artist left SAMO© behind, his art continued to reflect influences of the city, to which he added the African, French, and Latin traditions of his parents' homelands.

Anything and everything found its way into Basquiat's paintings: words and images from television, movies, parties, politics, jazz, sports, and Basquiat's collections of books, films, old photographs, rare toys, and other artists' works. Characteristically, the words could take on poetic meaning, make up a reference list, or describe something not seen. Many images—such as teeth, crowns, and arrows—were frequently repeated and became identified with his work. His characters were often stick figures, and his chalky backgrounds were reminiscent of SAMO©'s walls.

Basquiat's paintings are big, and he used paint, oil stick, pastels, and ink to make them. He made collages, painted, and drew on many different surfaces, from doors, window frames, and canvases crudely tied and nailed together to the classic artist's materials of paper and stretched canvas.

The artist's powerful pictures are humorous, angry, and sad. In them critics see connections to many of the great artists of this century—Jean Dubuffet, Jasper Johns, and Wilhelm de Kooning, even Pablo Picasso. Literary references can also be found both in the paintings and in their titles. Basquiat's great talent was to weave together the rhythms and textures of the city and the techniques and traditions of the fine arts.

The art world quickly discovered Basquiat, and the artist loved his success and the attention it brought him. In triumph, Basquiat surprised his father the morning after his first major New York gallery opening by arriving at his Brooklyn home in a stretch limousine. Beyond this kind of parading, Basquiat viewed success as being counted among the fine artists whose art reflected contemporary issues. In 1984, when the Museum of Modern Art in New York reopened after four years of remodeling, Basquiat's art was prominently exhibited in the inaugural show.

Basquiat was passionate and generous. He frequently gave away his drawings and paintings. He treasured his friends and never forgot a debt. Known as the "wild child," however, he led a fast life which took its toll. He used illegal drugs and went back and forth between "cures" and periods of drug-induced "highs." Basquiat's life was cut short when, in 1988, at the age of twenty-seven, he died of an accidental drug overdose in his studio.

Jean-Michel Basquiat's works show the world as the artist perceived it: crowded, funny, raucous, and scary—and always real.

SELECTED MUSEUMS WHERE JEAN-MICHEL BASQUIAT'S WORKS MAY BE SEEN:

EVERSON MUSEUM OF ART, *Syracuse, NY*
SOLOMON R. GUGGENHEIM MUSEUM, *New York, NY*
MUSEUM OF MODERN ART, *New York, NY*
WHITNEY MUSEUM OF AMERICAN ART, *New York, NY*
MUSEUM OF CONTEMPORARY ART, *Chicago, IL*
THE MUSEUM OF CONTEMPORARY ART, *Los Angeles, CA*
THE MENIL COLLECTION, *Houston, TX*

NORTON GALLERY OF ART, *West Palm Beach, FL*
MUSEUM OF FINE ARTS, *Montreal, Canada*
KESTNER-GESELLSCHAFT, *Hannover, Germany*
MUSEUM BOYMANS-VAN BEUNINGEN, *Rotterdam, The Netherlands*
MUSÉE CANTINI, *Marseille, France*
MUSÉE D'ART CONTEMPORAIN, *Pully, Switzerland*
SETAGAYA MUSEUM, *Tokyo, Japan*

For Morgan and Lily Kate
—S. J. B.

Designed by Paul Zakris

Published in 1993 by Stewart, Tabori & Chang
575 Broadway, New York, New York 10012

Library of Congress Cataloging-in-Publication Data
Angelou, Maya.
    Life doesn't frighten me / by Maya Angelou ;
paintings by Jean-Michel Basquiat ; edited by Sara
Jane Boyers.
        p. cm.
    Includes bibliographical references.
    Summary: Presents Maya Angelou's poem illustrated
by paintings and drawings of Jean-Michel Basquiat.
Features biographies of both author and artist.
    ISBN 1-55670-288-4
    1. Fear—Juvenile poetry. 2. Children's poetry,
American. [1. Fear—Poetry. 2. American poetry.
3. Angelou, Maya. 4. Authors, American. 5. Afro-
Americans—Biography. 6. Basquiat, Jean Michel.
7. Artists.] I. Basquiat, Jean Michel, ill. II. Boyers,
Sara Jane. III. Title.
PS3551.N464L54   1993
811'.54—dc20   92-40409
                                                CIP

Distributed in Canada by Canadian Manda Group,
P.O. Box 920 Station U, Toronto, Ontario, M8Z 5P9

Distributed in all other territories by
Melia Publishing Services, P.O. Box 1639,
Maidenhead, Berkshire, SL6 6YZ England

Printed in Singapore
10 9 8 7 6 5 4 3

The editor would like to thank Gérard Basquiat; the Estate
of Jean-Michel Basquiat; Robert Miller, John Cheim, and
Diana Bulman and the Robert Miller Gallery; Galerie Bruno
Bischofberger, Zurich; the office of Dr. Maya Angelou;
Morgan & Lily Kate, editorial; Leslie Rubin, research.

Illustration credits: Front jacket and page 11: *Pez Dispenser*
(1984), Oil on canvas, Private collection, Geneva, Switzerland,
Courtesy of the Estate of Jean-Michel Basquiat, Robert
Miller Gallery, New York and Enrico Navarra Gallery, Paris;
page 2: *Masque* (n.d.), Oil on canvas, 56 × 49½", Private
collection; page 5: *Untitled* (1982), Acrylic and oilstick on
canvas, 68 × 60", Private collection, Paris, Courtesy Galerie
Templon, Paris; pages 6–7: *Boy & Dog in a Johnnypump*
(1982), Acrylic on canvas, 94.4 × 165", Courtesy Galerie
Bruno Bischofberger, Zurich; pages 8–9: *Untitled* (1982),
70.8 × 150", Courtesy Galerie Bruno Bischofberger and the
Estate of Jean-Michel Basquiat, Courtesy of Robert Miller
Gallery, New York; page 10: *Untitled* (1981), Wax crayon on
paper, 12.2 × 17.3", By Courtesy of Didier Imbert Fine Art,
Paris; pages 12–13: *Self-Portrait* (1982), Synthetic polymer
paint and oilstick on linen, 76 × 94", Collection of Bo Franzen,
New York; page 15: *World Crown Series* (1981), Acrylic and
spraypaint on canvas, 56 × 47", Collection of Maggie Bult,
New York; pages 16–17: *Untitled* (n.d.), Acrylic and chalk
on paper, 14 × 23", Collection of Fausto Galeazzi, Brescia,
Italy; page 17: *Untitled* (1984), Acrylic and oilstick on canvas,
72 × 56¼", Courtesy of the Estate of Jean-Michel Basquiat,
Robert Miller Gallery, New York; pages 18–19: *Profit 1* (1982),
Acrylic on canvas, 86.5 × 157.5", Private collection, Courtesy
Galerie Bruno Bischofberger, Zurich; page 20: *Snakeman*
(1982/83), Mixed media on paper, 22.4 × 30.1", Courtesy
Thomas Ammann, Zurich; page 22: *Thirty-sixth Figure*
(n.d.), 60 × 47⅞", Private collection, Courtesy Galerie
Bruno Bischofberger and the Estate of Jean-Michel
Basquiat, Courtesy of Robert Miller Gallery, New York;
page 23: *Formless* (1982/83), Mixed media on paper,
22.4 × 30.1", Courtesy Thomas Ammann, Zurich; page 24:
Untitled (1983), Crayon on paper, 39.4 × 22.5", Courtesy
Galerie Bruno Bischofberger, Zurich; page 27: *Ass Killer*
(1984), Acrylic and oil on canvas, 66.1 × 59.8", Private
collection, Courtesy Galerie Bruno Bischofberger, Zurich;
page 28: © Nancy Robinson; page 30: © Lizzie Himmel